DONNA KOOLER'S
555 CROSS-STITCH
SAMPLER MOTIFS

DONNA KOOLER'S
555 CROSS-STITCH
SAMPLER MOTIFS

Donna Kooler

LARK BOOKS
A Division of Sterling Publishing Co., Inc.
New York / London

SENIOR EDITOR:
RAY HEMACHANDRA

PRODUCTION EDITOR:
LINDA KOPP

ART DIRECTORS:
MEGAN KIRBY AND
DANA IRWIN

SAMPLER ILLUSTRATORS:
PRISCILLA TIMM AND
MARIA PARRISH

PHOTOGRAPHER:
KEN PITTS

STITCH ILLUSTRATOR:
ORRIN LUNDGREN

COVER DESIGNER:
CINDY LABREACHT

EDITORIAL ASSISTANCE:
AMANDA CARESTIO

EDITORIAL INTERN:
HALLEY LAWRENCE

Library of Congress Cataloging-in-Publication Data

Kooler, Donna.
  Donna Kooler's 555 cross-stitch sampler motifs / Donna Kooler.
    p. cm.
  Includes index.
  ISBN-13: 978-1-60059-192-1 (HC-PLC with jkt. : alk. paper)
  ISBN-10: 1-60059-192-2 (HC-PLC with jkt. : alk. paper)
  1. Cross-stitch--Patterns. 2. Samplers. I. Title. II. Title: Donna
Kooler's five hundred fifty-five cross-stitch sampler motifs. III. Title:
555 cross-stitch sampler motifs.
  TT778.C76K66626 2008
  746.44'3041--dc22

                              2008000636

10 9 8 7 6 5 4 3 2

Published by Lark Books, A Division of
Sterling Publishing Co., Inc.
387 Park Avenue South, New York, NY 10016

Text © 2008, Donna Kooler
Sampler Illustrations © 2008, Donna Kooler
Photography © 2008, Lark Books unless otherwise specified
Stitch Illustrations © 2008, Lark Books unless otherwise specified

Distributed in Canada by Sterling Publishing,
c/o Canadian Manda Group, 165 Dufferin Street
Toronto, Ontario, Canada M6K 3H6

Distributed in the United Kingdom by GMC Distribution Services,
Castle Place, 166 High Street, Lewes, East Sussex, England BN7 1XU

Distributed in Australia by Capricorn Link (Australia) Pty Ltd.,
P.O. Box 704, Windsor, NSW 2756 Australia

If you have questions or comments about this book, please contact:
Lark Books
67 Broadway
Asheville, NC 28801
828-253-0467

Manufactured in China

ISBN 13: 978-1-60059-192-1

For information about custom editions, special sales, and premium and corporate purchases, please contact the Sterling Special Sales Department at 800-805-5489 or specialsales@sterlingpub.com.

CONTENTS

INTRODUCTION   6

THE BASICS   8

THE SAMPLERS

LOVE TAKES FLIGHT   10

NATURE'S WISDOM   22

FAMILY FIRST   36

A GAL'S BEST FRIENDS   50

SOUTH OF THE BORDER FIESTA   62

SIMPLE BLESSINGS   76

ALL CREATURES GREAT AND SMALL   86

HOME FOR THE HOLIDAYS   100

ALPHABET GARDEN   114

ANCHOR CONVERSION CHART   124

ACKNOWLEDGMENTS   126

ABOUT THE AUTHOR   126

METRIC CONVERSION CHART   127

INDEX   127

INTRODUCTION

ONCE UPON A TIME, stitching was an everyday activity for most women. While noblewomen and queens and their ladies stitched pretty motifs—letters, trees, flowers, animals, people, and anything else they could dream up—to brighten their environs and their afternoons, common women took a more practical approach to cross-stitch.

They stitched samplers of alphabets and stylized motifs on squares of linen and then onto their other valued fabric possessions, so their sheets, towels, and garments wouldn't be mistaken for a neighbor's. These women also recognized that carefully stitched, colorful patterns were beautiful in their own right, and they often hung samplers in their homes for decoration as well as reference.

You can make this ancient art new—and your own. We all enjoy creating beautiful things in our precious leisure time. It is satisfying to look at a sampler and see a bright reminder of the time we spent creating it. Stitching is a very personal way to record milestone events, such as weddings, births, graduations, and anniversaries. Enormous pleasure can be found in stitching a family heirloom or a gift for a friend's special day. When other people enjoy our work, our delight only grows.

What subjects make your heart leap? Our nine samplers include an array of themes and motifs from family and holidays to butterflies and flowers. Accessorize your bedroom with a sampler featuring hats, purses, and shoes (page 50). Simple Blessings, stitched entirely in red thread, is a tribute to peace and simplicity (page 76), while the beauty and vivacity of Latino culture are celebrated in brilliant style on a dark background in South of the Border Fiesta (page 62). Animal lovers will enjoy paying tribute to a special dog or cat—as well as beloved fish, bunnies, and hamsters—with the All Creatures Great and Small sampler (page 86).

Make your own mark in history using these twenty-first century motifs. I've provided plenty of alternative images—more than 555 motifs between the sampler and the alternatives—so you can customize each sampler to reflect your own experiences and treasured loved ones.

I hope you find endless delight in making these samplers, and that the beautiful works your hands create live on and on. Cross-stitched projects can provide the perfect touch of handcrafted elegance for your home, as warm and loving as a caress. Let your stitching remind the world—for generations—of the most beautiful things in life.

Enjoy, *Donna Kooler*

THE BASICS

READY TO EMBARK on a timeless craft dating back to the fifteenth century? Samplers are the world's oldest form of embroidery, and this book contains a colorful collection of patterns that will help you create your very own cross-stitch masterpieces. Each design includes alternate patterns, so you can personalize your project with a number of design and color options. Getting started is easy. All you need is a few supplies and some basic stitches.

FABRIC

Even-weave fabrics are almost always used for counted cross-stitch. These fabrics are created specifically for this kind of embroidery and have the same number of horizontal and vertical threads per inch. Because the fabric has an equal number of threads vertically and horizontally, each stitch is the same size. The size of the finished design is determined by the number of threads per inch.

PREPARING THE FABRIC

To make sure you have plenty of space to work and finish the edges comfortably, cut the fabric so it's at least 3 inches (7.6 cm) larger on all sides than the finished design size. If you are creating your design as part of a more complicated project, check the pattern instructions for the proper fabric allowance. To prevent the fabric from fraying, you should zigzag stitch (with a sewing machine) or whipstitch along any raw edges; you could also apply liquid fray preventer.

CENTERING THE DESIGN

To center the design on your cross-stitch fabric, fold the fabric in half horizontally, then vertically. Push a pin into the fold point to mark the center of the fabric. Next, find the center of the design on the graph. To help find the center of the design, arrows are provided at the left center and top center. Begin stitching your design at the center point of both the graph and fabric.

FINISHED DESIGN SIZE

You can determine the size of a finished design by dividing the stitch count by the number of threads per inch of fabric. When the design is stitched over two threads, divide the stitch count by half the threads per inch.

CLEANING YOUR WORK

You may find it necessary to clean your finished design. Start by soaking the fabric in cold water with a mild soap for five to 10 minutes. Rinse the piece well and then roll it in a towel to remove the excess water, being careful not to wring the fabric. Place the piece face down on a dry towel, and iron it on a warm setting until the fabric is dry.

FLOSS

Each sampler and design graph is coded with colors and numbers that represent DMC floss colors (Anchor conversion chart is located on page 124). You'll want to use 18-inch (45.7 cm) lengths of floss for your designs, separating the strands for the best coverage. Use a wet sponge to dampen the floss, and then put together the number of strands needed for the fabric you're using.

NUMBER OF STRANDS

The number of strands used per inch varies depending on what fabric you decide to use. When cross-stitching, you can use these general rules: three strands on Aida 11; two strands on Aida 14; one or two on Aida 18 (depending on how thick you want the stitches to be); and one strand on Hardanger 22.

When backstitching, use just one strand on all fabrics. When stitching a French knot, use two strands and one wrap on all fabrics.

CARRYING FLOSS

To carry the floss, weave it underneath the previously worked stitches on the back. Do not carry thread across any fabric that is not or will not be stitched. Loose threads, especially dark ones, will show through the fabric.

SECURING THE FLOSS

Never knot your floss unless you are working on clothing or making a waste knot. There are two ways to secure floss. The first is to insert your needle from the underside of the fabric at the starting point and, holding 1 inch (2.5 cm) of thread behind the fabric, stitch over the thread, securing it with the first few stitches. Finish securing the thread by running it under four or more stitches on the back of the design.

The second method is to make a waste knot. Do this by knotting the floss and then inserting the needle from the right side of the fabric, about 1 inch (2.5 cm) from the design area. Work a few stitches over the thread to secure it, then cut the knot off later.

NEEDLES

Needles should slip through fabric holes easily and without piercing the fabric threads. For fabric with 11 or fewer threads per inch, use a tapestry needle size 24; for 14 threads per inch, use a size 24 or 26; for 18 or more per inch, use a size 26. Don't leave the needle in the fabric; it may cause rust or a permanent impression.

STITCHES

Only a handful of simple stitches are needed to complete the samplers in this book. Refer to the steps on the facing page if a stitch is unfamiliar to you, or if you could use a refresher.

CROSS STITCH (X)

Choose one of the two methods of stitching:

- Complete each cross stitch individually (see middle of diagram), OR
- Stitch a row of half cross stitches, then complete each stitch on the return journey (top diagram). Make sure the top "leg" always crosses in the same direction.

The bottom illustration is an example of petite cross stitch, which is stitched over one intersection.

FRACTIONAL CROSS

There are three ways to make this stitch. Use one of the following stitch combinations:

- Two quarter crosses and then a backstitch (lower left in illustration)
- Two three-quarter crosses (lower center)
- One quarter cross and one three-quarter cross (lower right)

The top left illustration shows examples of quarter stitches, and the top right shows three-quarter stitches.

HALF CROSS

You may work from left to right (shown) or from right to left, and from top to bottom or from bottom to top.

BACKSTITCH (BS)

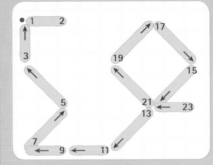

This stitch can be worked over any number of threads, most commonly over two, three, or four threads. Work from left to right, from right to left, vertically, or diagonally.

STRAIGHT (STR)

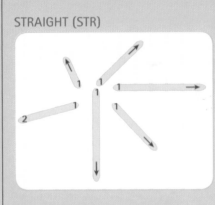

A single straight stitch can be worked in any direction over any number of threads. Bring the needle up at the point marked 1, then down at the point marked 2.

FRENCH KNOT (FK)

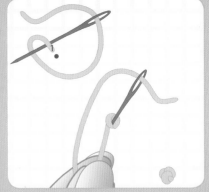

1 Wrap the thread around the needle once or twice, keeping the thread snug around the barrel of the needle. For larger or thicker French knots, you may increase the number of thread strands or the weight of the thread.

2 When inserting the needle back into the ground fabric, move one linen thread (or a partial Aida square) over from where the needle originally emerged to prevent the knot from slipping through the fabric to the back.

COLONIAL KNOT

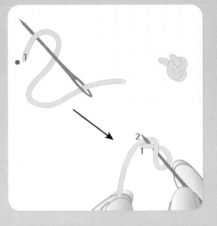

1 Bring your needle up through the fabric where you want the knot.

2 Wrap the thread around the needle in a figure eight fashion.

3 Keeping tension on the thread, push the needle back down through the fabric one linen thread (or a partial Aida square) over from where the needle first emerged.

LOVE
TAKES FLIGHT

Love Takes Flight

Size: 154w x 191h
Fabric: 14 ct. Charles Craft, White

DMC	X	BS
155	▫	
310	◨	⟋
333	✖	
352	Z	
503	◣	

DMC	X	BS
552	⬆	
606	Ⅱ	
666	◪	
733	4	
740	H	

Grayed stitches indicate last row from previous section of design.

Love Takes Flight

DMC	X	BS		DMC	X	BS
743	★			919	◣	
746	·			921	◎	
797	▲	⟋		3609	◥	
799	5			3805	▢	
800	✚			3820	⬢	
816	▣					

Love Takes Flight

DMC	X	BS		DMC	X	BS
155	▫			552	▲	
310	◨	✎		606	I	
333	✖			666	◧	
352	Z			733	4	
503	◣			740	H	

Grayed stitches indicate last row from previous section of design.

Love Takes Flight

DMC	X	BS		DMC	X	BS
743	★			919	◣	
746	·			921	○	
797	▲	⬭		3609	◥	
799	5			3805	◻	
800	✚			3820	⊥	
816	■					

Bottom Left

Love Takes Flight

DMC	X	BS		DMC	X	BS
155				552		
310				606		
333				666		
352				733		
503				740		

Grayed stitches indicate last row from previous section of design.

Love Takes Flight

DMC	X	BS		DMC	X	BS
743	★			919	◢	
746	·			921	○	
797	▲	◢		3609	◥	
799	5			3805	▢	
800	✚			3820	⊥	
816	▣					

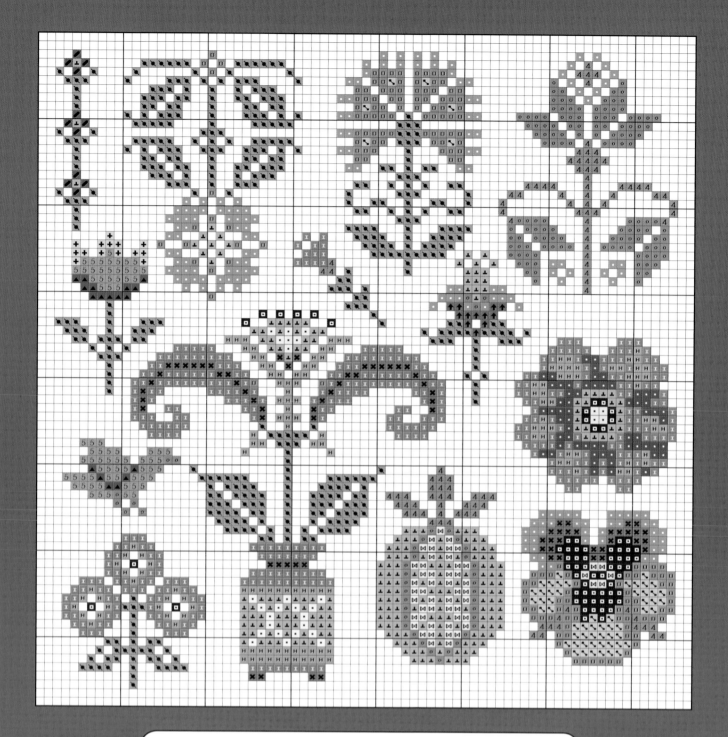

Love Takes Flight
Alternate Designs

DMC	X	BS
155	▪	
310	▣	✏
333	✖	
352	☑	
445	⊠	
503	◥	

DMC	X	BS
552	↑	
606	⊥	
733	4	
740	H	
746	▪	
797	▲	
799	5	

DMC	X	BS
800	✚	
816	▪	
919	◥	✏
921	○	
3609	◣	
3805	▢	
3820	⊥	

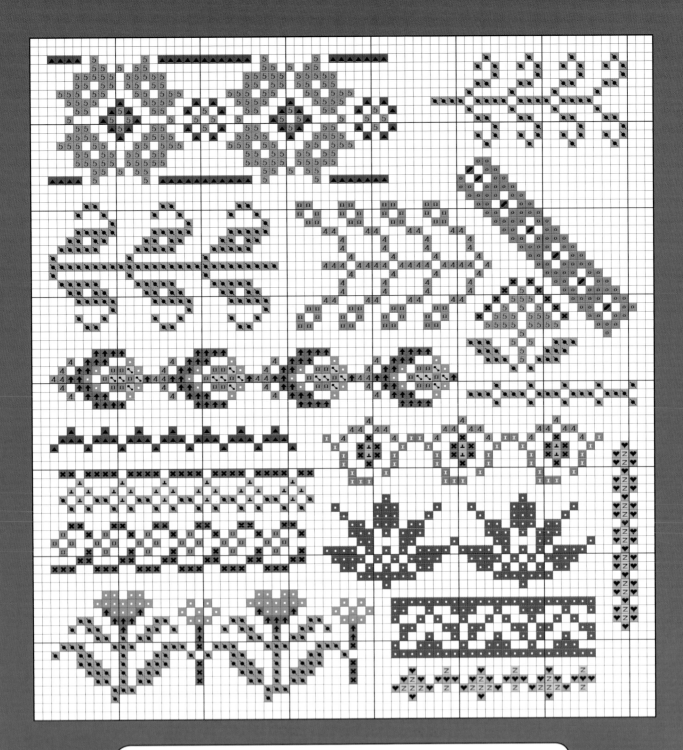

Love Takes Flight
Alternate Designs

DMC	X	BS		DMC	X	BS		DMC	X	BS
155	▪			552	⬆			799	5	
310	⊡			606	I			816	▪	
333	✖			666	◼			919	◢	◢
351	♥			733	4			921	○	
352	Z			740	H			3609	◥	
503	◣			746	·			3805	▫	
				797	▲	◢		3820	⊥	

NATURE'S
WISDOM

Nature's Wisdom

Size: 149w x 191h

Fabric: 14 ct. Charles Craft, White

DMC	X	BS		DMC	X	BS
1	◈			471	Z	
208	◖			501	▲	
209	△			502	7	
211	H			503	a	
320	⊥			519	⌐	
351	◿			554	4	
367	↑			727	▮	
433	✕			729	m	
435	◣			741	☆	
470	♠					

Grayed stitches indicate last row from previous section of design.

Nature's Wisdom

DMC	X	BS		DMC	X	BS
742	✖			3041	✚	✎ *
743	◇			3042	n	
772	C			3348	〉	
799	◖			3350	✖	
818	▬			3354	✛	
828	o			3731	◗	
838	◼	✎ *		3743	☐	
921	◆			3746	◧	
962	e			3803	♥	
989	✕			3823	∾	

*2-ply

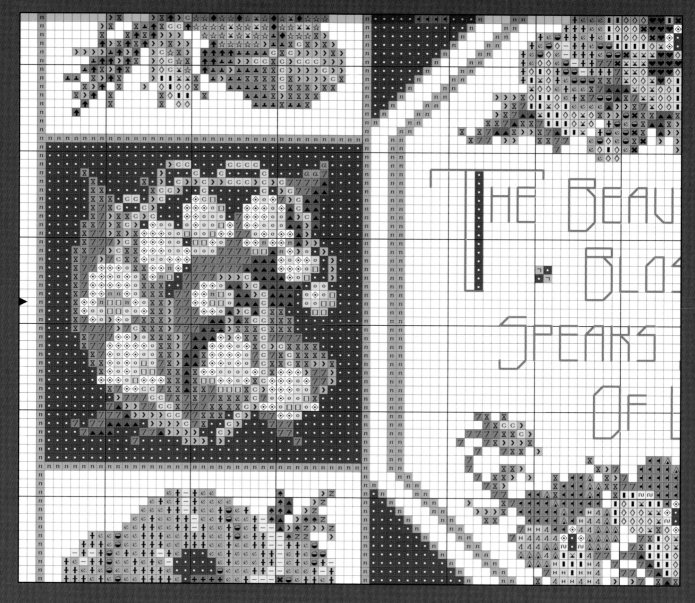

Nature's Wisdom

DMC	X	BS		DMC	X	BS
1	◈			471	Z	
208	◀			501	▲	
209	◮			502	7	
211	H			503	a	
320	⊥			519	⌐	
351	◪			554	4	
367	⬆			727	▮	
433	✕			729	m	
435	↖			741	☆	
470	♠					

Grayed stitches indicate last row from previous section of design.

Nature's Wisdom

DMC	X	BS		DMC	X	BS
742	✖			3041	✚	⬭ *
743	◇			3042	n	
772	C			3348	❯	
799	◣			3350	✖	
818	―			3354	✚	
828	o			3731	◖	
838	▪	⬭ *		3743	▢	
921	◆			3746	▣	
962	e			3803	♥	
989	✕			3823	∿	

*2-ply

Nature's Wisdom

DMC	X	BS		DMC	X	BS
1	◈			471	Z	
208	◀			501	▲	
209	◭			502	7	
211	H			503	a	
320	⊥			519	⌐	
351	◿			554	4	
367	↑			727	❙	
433	✕			729	m	
435	◥			741	☆	
470	♠					

Nature's Wisdom

DMC	X	BS		DMC	X	BS
742	✖			3041	✚	⬭ *
743	◇			3042	n	
772	C			3348	❯	
799	◣			3350	✖	
818	─			3354	✚	
828	o			3731	◓	
838	▪	⬭ *		3743	□	
921	◆			3746	◩	
962	e			3803	♥	
989	✗			3823	∾	

*2-ply

29

JANUARY
Carnation

FEBRUARY
Violet

ABCDEFGHIJKLMNOP
QRSTUVWXYZ

ABCDEFGHIJKLMN
OPQRSTUVWXYZ
1234567890

APRIL · MAY · JUNE
Daisy Lily of the Valley Rose

Nature's Wisdom
Alternate Designs

DMC	X	1/4	BS	FK	DMC	X	1/4	BS	FK	DMC	X	1/4	BS	FK	DMC	X	1/4	BS	FK
1	◈				501	▪				743	I				3348	❭			
208	◀				502	♡			● *	772	C		C		3350	✖			
209	▲				503	a				799	◣				3354	‡			
211	H				519	7				818	☆				3731	◖			
320	◣				727	⧺				838	▣		╱	●	3746	◇◇			
367	◢				729	m				962	e				3813	V			
435	◥				741	★				989	⊠				3823	∿			● *
471	♠				742	⊠				3346	●								

*2-ply

Note: For flowers corresponding to April, May, and June, use sampler chart on previous pages.

· AUGUST ·

Gladiolus

SEPTEMBER

· Aster ·

Johnny-jump-up

Tulip

Morning Glory

Sunflower

Hydrangea

DECEMBER

· Poinsettia ·

Oriental Poppy

Nature's Wisdom
Alternate Designs

DMC	X	1/4	BS	STR	FK	DMC	X	1/4	BS	STR	FK	DMC	X	1/4	BS	STR	FK
1	◈					502	7				• *	962	e				
208	◀					503	a					989	X				
209	◬					554	4					3042	n				
211	H					727	▌					3326	◧				
320	⊥					729	m					3348	❭				
351	◩					741	☆					3350	✖				•
352	⌐					742	✕					3731	◓				
367	▲					743	◇					3743	▫				
433	⊠					772	C	C				3803	♥				
435	◤					818	—					3823	∿				⬭
471	Z					838			⬭		•						
501	▲					921	◆										

*2-ply

Nature's Wisdom
Alternate Designs

DMC	X	BS		DMC	X	BS		DMC	X	BS	FK		DMC	X	BS
1	◈			435	◥			742	✕				3042	n	✎
208	◀			471	Z			743	◇				3348	❭	
209	◭			501	▲			772	C				3350	✖	
211	H			502	7			818	−				3354	✚	
320	⊥			503	a			838	■	✎	•		3731	◓	
351	◪			554	4			962	e				3743	□	
352	⌐			727	▮			989	✗				3803	♥	
367	⬆			729	m			3041	✛				3823	∿	
433	✕			741	☆										

35

FAMILY FIRST

Babies are Special

Personalization Line

Family First

Size: 153w x 195h
Fabric: 14 ct. Charles Craft , Blush

DMC	X	BS	FK	DMC	X	BS	FK	DMC	X	BS	FK	DMC	X	BS	FK
1	◈			351	◭	✎ *		758	⑤			3608	✚		
164	∩			352	◕			803	♡			3609	C		
169	♣			353	H			816	♥			3712	✚		
208	★			402	⚓			899	2			3755	m		
210	T			433	⬆	✎ *		910	◼	✎ *	•	3770	ɪ		
310	▣	✎	•	435	◣			912	✖			3776	♠		
312	o	✎ *		702	◖			954	◭			3820	▲		
319	✕	✎ *	•	704	③			955	Z			3841	⊥		
334	◤	✎ *		722	⑥			3325	◀			3856	⌐		
347	⑨			743	L			3326	V						
350	⌘			744	☆			3348	n						

Grayed stitches indicate last row from previous section of design.

Two Shall Become One

39

Family First

DMC	X	BS	FK
1	◈		
164	∩		
169	♣		
208	★		
210	T		
310	▣	✎	●
312	o	✎ *	
319	✕	✎ *	●
334	✎	✎ *	
347	9		
350	⌘		

DMC	X	BS	FK
351	⏶	✎ *	
352	◣		
353	H		
402	⬇		
433	⬆	✎ *	
435	◣		
702	◑		
704	3		
722	6		
743	L		
744	☆		

DMC	X	BS	FK
758	S		
803	♡		
816	♥		
899	2		
910	■	✎ *	●
912	✕		
954	A		
955	Z		
3325	◀		
3326	V		
3348	n		

DMC	X	BS	FK
3608	✚		
3609	C		
3712	✚		
3755	m		
3770	I		
3776	♠		
3820	▲		
3841	⊥		
3856	⌐		

Personalization Line   *2-ply

Grayed stitches indicate last row from previous section of design.

Personalization Line

Personalization Line

Personalization Line

Home is where the heart is

Family First

DMC	X	BS	FK	DMC	X	BS	FK	DMC	X	BS	FK	DMC	X	BS	FK
1	◈			351	◭	✎ *		758	⑤			3608	✚		
164	∩			352	◥			803	♡			3609	C		
169	♣			353	H			816	♥			3712	✚		
208	★			402	⚓			899	②			3755	m		
210	T			433	⬆	✎ *		910	◧	✎ *	•	3770	⌶		
310	◘	✎	•	435	◣			912	✕			3776	♠		
312	o	✎ *		702	◗			954	⋀			3820	▲		
319	✕	✎ *	•	704	③			955	Z			3841	⊥		
334	◢	✎ *		722	⑥			3325	◖			3856	⌐		
347	⑨			743	L			3326	V						
350	⌘			744	☆			3348	⒩						

Personalization Line   *2-ply

Grayed stitches indicate last row from previous section of design.

Personalization Line

Personalization Line

Personalization Line

A Brother Shares
Size: 71w x 93h

DMC	X	BS	FK	DMC	X	BS	FK
1	◈			435	◥		
310	▣	•		436	⊥		
312	⊙	✎ *		816	♥		
334	✕			910	▣		
350	⌘			3325	◢		
352	◥			3712	✚		
433	⬆						

Personalization Line   *2-ply

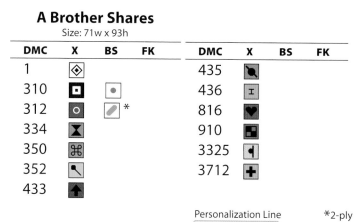

my ❀ ❀ my
Sister Friend

Personalization Line

My Sister My Friend
Size: 73w x 95h

DMC	X	BS	FK
208	★		
210	T		
309	◆	✎ *	•
310	▣		
312	○		
334	✕		

DMC	X	BS	FK
335	✕		
350	⌘		
351	△		
352	◣		
433	⬆		•
435	◥		
436	⊥		
783	m		

DMC	X	BS	FK
816	♥		
899	2		
912	⊠		
954	▲		
3325	◀		
3326	V		
3712	✚		
3856	⌐		

Personalization Line   *2-ply

Dads Are Special
Size: 73w x 95h

DMC	X	BS	FK		DMC	X	BS	FK
310	▣		●		743	L		
312	◎				783	m	╱ *	
334	✖	╱ *			816	♥		
350	⌘				910	◪		
433	▲	╱ *	●		912	✕		
435	◣				920	⬇		

Personalization Line   *2-ply

Mom Is Another Word for Love

Size: 77w x 97h

DMC	X	BS	FK	DMC	X	BS	FK	DMC	X	BS	FK
208	★			351	◭			912	⊠		
210	T			352	◣			954	▲		
309	◆	╱	*	436	ɪ			3325	◀		
334	⊠	╱	*	899	2			3326	V		
335	⊠			910	▦			3856	˥		

Personalization Line   *2-ply

OUR FIRST HOME

center street

center city

center name   center name

EST   date

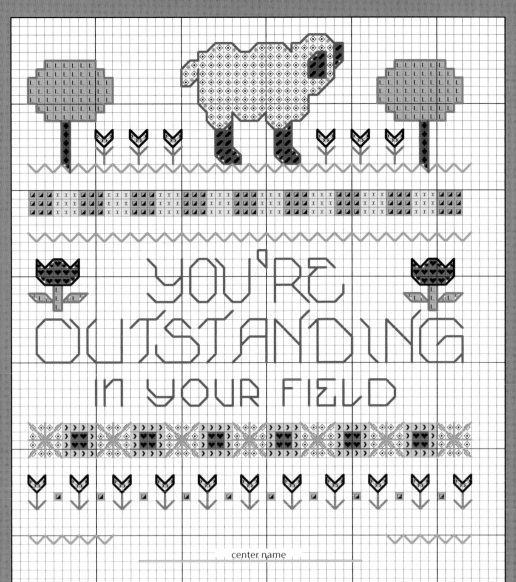

YOU'RE OUTSTANDING IN YOUR FIELD

center name

ABCDEFGHIJKLMNOPQRSTUVWXYZ
1234567890

Family First
Alternate Designs

DMC	X	1/4	BS		DMC	X	1/4	BS
100	◈	◈			562	↑	↑	╱
309	♥	♥	╱		744	I		
368	L	L			754	H	H	
413	╱	╱	╱		775	▪		╱
433	◆	◆	╱		776	❯	❯	
435	⊥	⊥			794	◢		

Personalization Line

A GAL'S
BEST FRIENDS

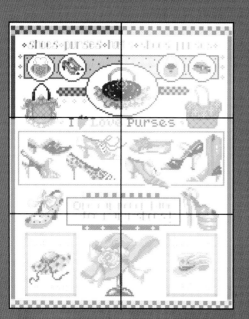

A Gal's Best Friends
Size: 155w x 197h
Fabric: 14 ct. Charles Craft, White

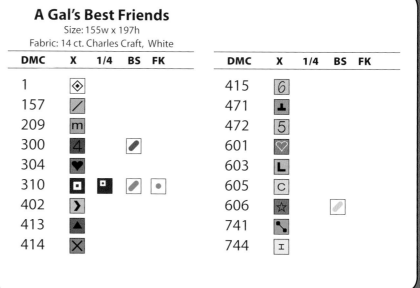

DMC	X	1/4	BS	FK
1	◈			
157	∕			
209	m			
300	4		⬗	
304	♥			
310	▣	▣	⬗	•
402	❯			
413	▲			
414	✕			

DMC	X	1/4	BS	FK
415	6			
471	⬩			
472	5			
601	♡			
603	L			
605	C			
606	☆		⬗	
741	↘			
744	I			

Grayed stitches indicate last row from previous section of design.

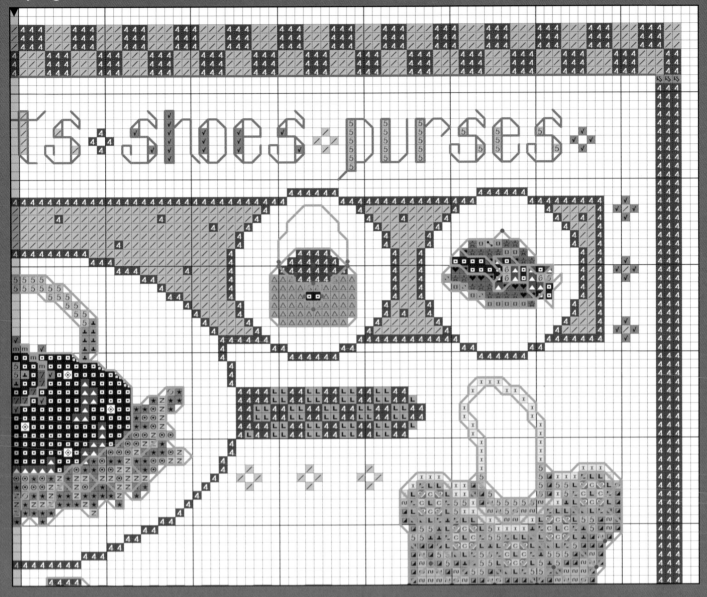

A Gal's Best Friends

DMC	X	1/4	BS	FK	DMC	X	1/4	BS	FK
775					970				
783					972				
791					3607				
798					3608				
799					3609				
907					3805				
919					3821				
921					3837				
945					3846				

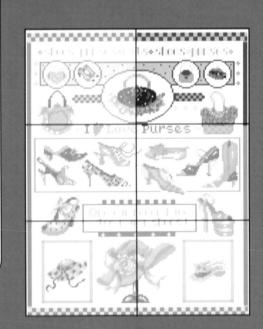

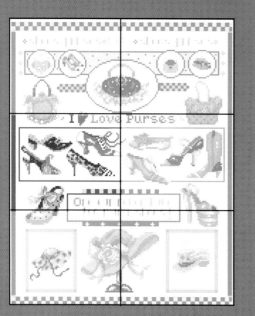

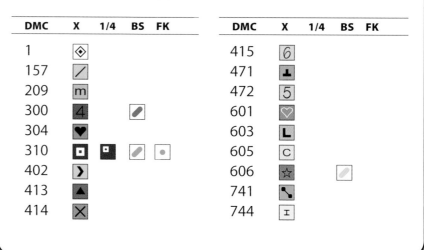

A Gal's Best Friends

DMC	X	1/4	BS	FK		DMC	X	1/4	BS	FK
1	◈					415	6			
157	╱					471	⊥			
209	m					472	5			
300	4		▱			601	♡			
304	♥		▱			603	L			
310	▣	▣	▱	•		605	C			
402	❭					606	☆		▱	
413	▲					741	◣			
414	✕					744	I			

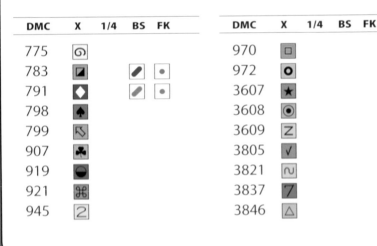

A Gal's Best Friends

DMC	X	1/4	BS	FK
775	⌒			
783	◩		✎	•
791	◆		✎	•
798	♠			
799	⬊			
907	♣			
919	◖			
921	⌘			
945	2			

DMC	X	1/4	BS	FK
970	▢			
972	◉			
3607	★			
3608	◉			
3609	Z			
3805	√			
3821	∼			
3837	7			
3846	△			

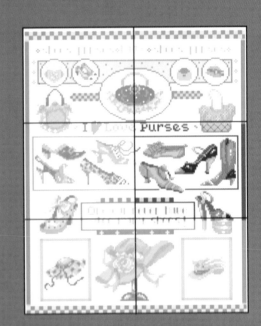

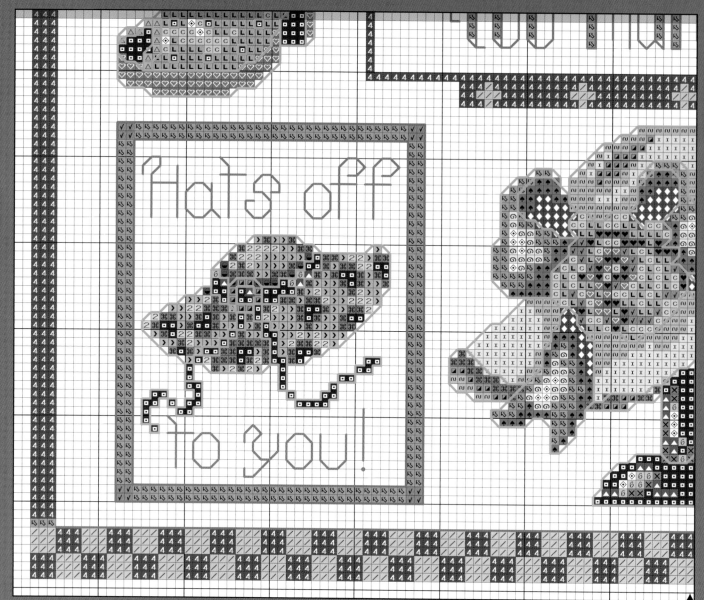

A Gal's Best Friends

DMC	X	1/4	BS	FK	DMC	X	1/4	BS	FK
1	◈				415	6			
157	/				471	⊥			
209	m				472	5			
300	4		╱		601	♥			
304	♥				603	L			
310	▣	▣	╱	•	605	C			
402	❯				606	☆		╱	
413	▲				741	↘			
414	✕				744	I			

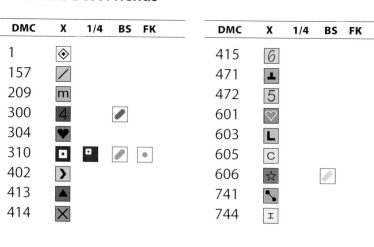

Grayed stitches indicate last row from previous section of design.

A Gal's Best Friends

DMC	X	1/4	BS	FK
775	⟲			
783	◨		╱	•
791	◆		╱	•
798	♠			
799	⬚			
907	♣			
919	⬤			
921	⌘			
945	2			

DMC	X	1/4	BS	FK
970	☐			
972	⊙			
3607	★			
3608	⊙			
3609	Z			
3805	✓			
3821	∾			
3837	7			
3846	△			

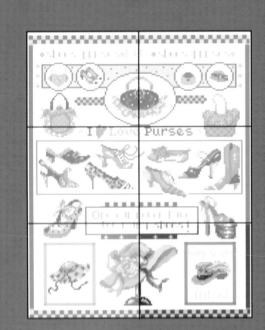

57

A Gal's Best Friends
Alternate Designs

DMC	X	BS	FK
1	◈		
209	m		
304	♥		
310	▣	╱	•
333	◀		
340	O		
341	a		
351	◀		
352	3		
402	❯		
413	▲		

DMC	X	BS
414	✕	
415	6	
472	5	
498	◆◆	
550	◢	
563	●	
601	♡	
603	L	
605	C	
606	☆	╱
741	◣	

DMC	X	BS
744	ᴵ	
783	◨	
913	8	
920	✕	
921	⌘	
945	2	
955	✕	
964	III	
970	▢	
972	◉	

DMC	X	BS	FK
3011	H		
3012	$		
3607	★		
3608	◉		
3609	Z		
3805	√		
3821	∾		•
3835	◕		
3837	7		
3846	△		•

A Gal's Best Friends
Alternate Designs

DMC	X	BS	DMC	X	DMC	X	DMC	X	DMC	X	FK
1	◈		402	❯	606	☆	806	➡	972	◉	
209	m		413	▲	702	T	807	n	3607	★	
300		✎	414	✕	741	◥	907	♣	3608	⊙	▫
304	♥		415	6	744	I	911	⧻	3609	Z	
310	▣	✎	472	5	747	■	913	8	3766	H	
333	◀		498	◆◆	775	⌒	920	✕	3807	◨	
340	○		550	◿	783	◪	921	⌘	3821	∽	
341	a		563	●	791	◆	945	2	3835	◓	
350	✚		601	♡	794	∨	955	⊠	3836	⁞	
351	◖		603	L	798	♠	964	Ⅲ	3837	7	
352	3		605	C	799	◖	970	▢	3846	△	

South of the Border
FIESTA

South of the Border Fiesta

Size: 155w x 194h
Fabric: 14 ct. Charles Craft, Black

DMC	X	1/4	BS	FK		DMC	X	1/4	BS	FK
1	◈	◇		• *		603	T			
155	8					605	♡			
209	I					608	∧	∧	▱	•
304	●		▱			608			▱	*
310	▣	▣	▱	•		666	◢			
333	♠					740	◣	◣		
356	⊠					741	—	—		
472	❮					742	★	★		
598	⊞					743	•	•		
602	◤					744	◀			

*2-ply

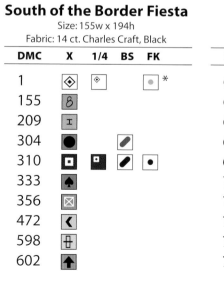
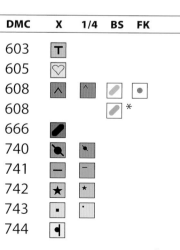

64

Grayed stitches indicate last row from previous section of design.

South of the Border Fiesta

DMC	X	1/4	BS	FK		DMC	X	1/4	BS	FK
758	—					3830	◆			
796	■					3837	✚			
798	L	L				3841	e			
905	⬆					3844	◢		⬜	
906	♥	♥				3844			✎	*
907	◓	◓				3846	o	o		
3607	✕					3849	◆			
3608	◇					3853	⌐		✎	*
3755	♥	♥								
3778	o									

*2-ply

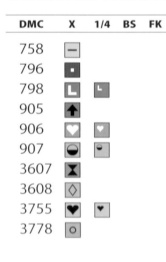

South of the Border Fiesta

DMC	X	1/4	BS	FK		DMC	X	1/4	BS	FK
1	◈	◇		● *		603	T			
155	8					605	♡			
209	I					608	^	^	⁄	•
304	●		⁄			608			⁄	*
310	▣	▣	⁄	•		666	◣			
333	♠					740	◣	◣		
356	⊠					741	—	—		
472	‹					742	★	★		
598	⊞					743	•	•		
602	⬆					744	◂			

*2-ply

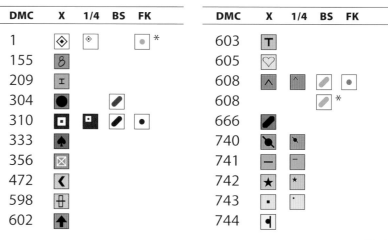

South of the Border Fiesta

DMC	X	1/4	BS	FK
758	—			
796	■			
798	L	L		
905	↑			
906	♥	♥		
907	◖	◔		
3607	✕			
3608	◇			
3755	♥	♥		
3778	○			

DMC	X	1/4	BS	FK
3830	◆			
3837	✚			
3841	e			
3844	◢		╱	
3844			╱	*
3846	○	◔		
3849	◆			
3853	⌐		╱	*

*2-ply

Bottom Left

South of the Border Fiesta

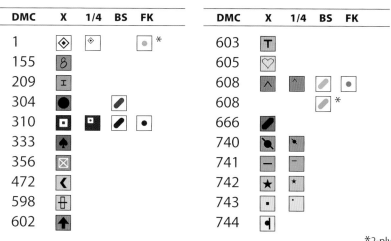

DMC	X	1/4	BS	FK		DMC	X	1/4	BS	FK
1	◈	◈		● *		603	T			
155	8					605	♡			
209	I					608	∧	∧	⬧	●
304	●		◢			608			◢ *	
310	▣	▣	◢	●		666			◢	
333	♠					740	◀	◥		
356	⊠					741	—	—		
472	◀					742	★	★		
598	⊞					743	·	·		
602	↑					744	◀			

*2-ply

South of the Border Fiesta

DMC	X	1/4	BS	FK
758	—			
796	■			
798	L	L		
905	♠			
906	♥	♥		
907	◖	◗		
3607	✕			
3608	◇			
3755	♥	♥		
3778	○			

DMC	X	1/4	BS	FK
3830	◆			
3837	✚			
3841	e			
3844	◢		╱	
3844			╱	*
3846	○	▫		
3849	◆			
3853	◥		╱	*

*2-ply

South of the Border Fiesta

Alternate Designs

DMC	X	1/4	BS	FK
1	◈			•
209	I			
310	▣	▪	╱	•
351	◪			
402	e			
472	<			
602	↑			
603	T			
604	▪			
608	^			
666	╱		╱	•
740	●			
741	H			
742	★			
743	▪			
744	◂			
758	—			
798	L			
904	♥		╱	
906	■			
907	◒			
911	—			
913	▪			
945	↑			
955	⊥			
3607	⧗			
3609	∧			
3778	o	°		
3830	◆		╱	
3837	+			
3844	⊿			
3846	o		╱	
3853	┐			

South of the Border Fiesta
Alternate Designs

DMC	X	1/4	BS	FK
1	◈			•
209	I			
211	Z			
310	⊡		⬙	•
351	◪			
352	△			
472	❮			
602	⬆			
603	T			
604	•			

DMC	X	1/4	BS	FK
608	∧			
666	◣		⬙	
740	◖			
741	H			
742	★			
743	•			
744	◀			
758	▬			
798	L			
904	♥		⬙	
906	■			
907	◐			

DMC	X	1/4	BS	FK
911	▬			
913	•			
945	↑			
955	⊥			
3607	✕			
3609	⋀			
3778	○			
3830	◆		⬙	
3837	✚			
3844	◿			
3846	○		⬙	
3853	⌐			

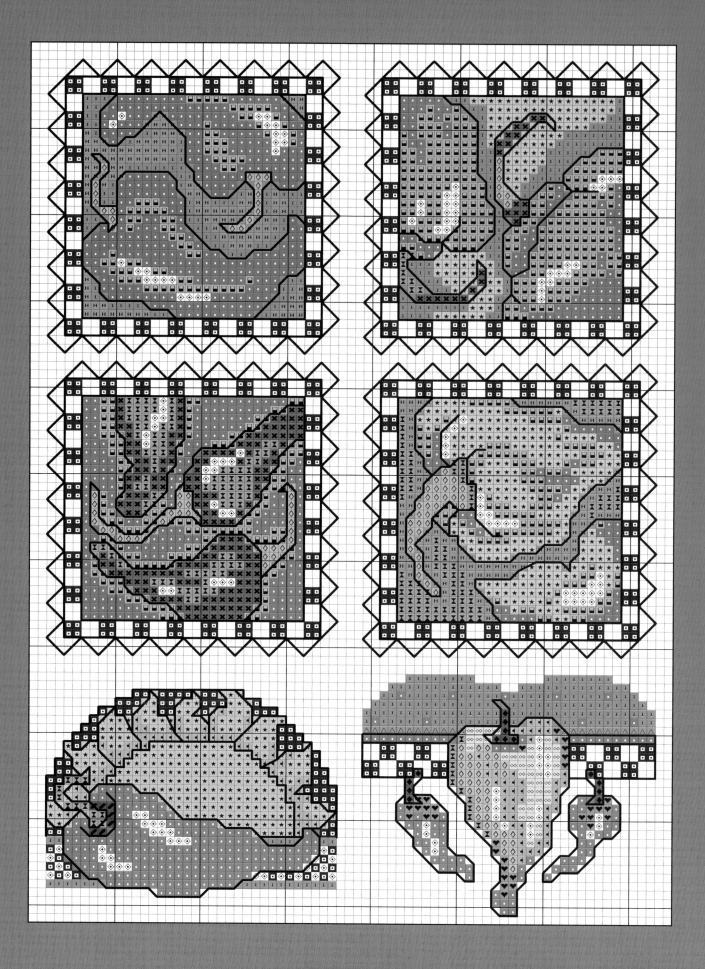

South of the Border Fiesta
Alternate Designs

DMC	X	1/4	BS	FK
1	◈			
208	I			
310	▣		✎	
445	T			
666	▪			
703	✕			
734	◕			
741	◀			
743	∞			
815	◣			

DMC	X	1/4	BS	FK
910	✖			
947	♥			
958	H			
972	★			
986	◆			
996	△			
3340	▢			
3348	◇			
3347	◣			

SIMPLE
BLESSINGS

Simple Blessings
Size: 149w x 191h
Fabric: 28 ct. Charles Craft, Tea-dyed Linen

DMC	X	BS
304	■	✎

Grayed stitches indicate last row from previous section of design.

Simple Blessings

DMC	X	BS
304		

Simple Blessings

DMC	X	BS
304	■	✏

Grayed stitches indicate last row from previous section of design.

Simple Blessings

DMC	X	BS
304	■	✎

Simple Blessings

DMC	X	BS
304	■	✎

Grayed stitches indicate last row from previous section of design.

Simple Blessings

DMC	X	BS
304	■	✎

Kind hearts are Gardens

Kind words are Flowers

Simple Blessings
Alternate Designs

DMC	X	BS
304	■	✎

ALL CREATURES
GREAT AND SMALL

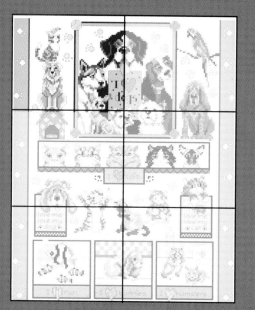

All Creatures Great and Small

Size: 155w x 197h
Fabric: 14 ct. Charles Craft, White

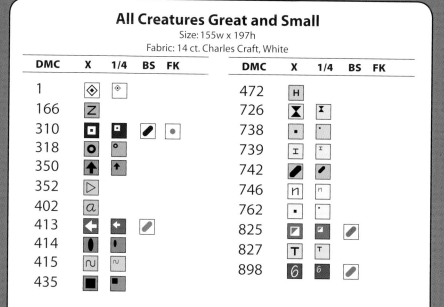

DMC	X	1/4	BS	FK	DMC	X	1/4	BS	FK
1	◈	◈			472	H			
166	Z				726	✕	✕		
310	◼	◼	⟋	•	738	•	•		
318	◉	◦			739	I	I		
350	⬆	⬆			742	⟋	⟋		
352	▷				746	n	n		
402	a				762	•	•		
413	◀	◀	⟋		825	◪	◪	⟋	
414	◖	◖			827	T	T		
415	~	~			898	6	6	⟋	
435	◼	◼							

Grayed stitches indicate last row from previous section of design.

All Creatures Great and Small

DMC	X	1/4	BS	FK
899	C	C		
906	—	—		
907	◣	◢		
921	◆	◆		
922	L	L		
975	4	4	⬭	
977	1	1		
3716	—	—		
3778	5	5		
3779	o	o		

DMC	X	1/4	BS	FK
3825	I	I		
3826	▪	▪		
3830	♥	♥		
3844	3	3		
3846	✖	✖		
3855	✚			
3858	◗	◗		
3862	▶			
3863	—	—		
3864	⋀	⋀		

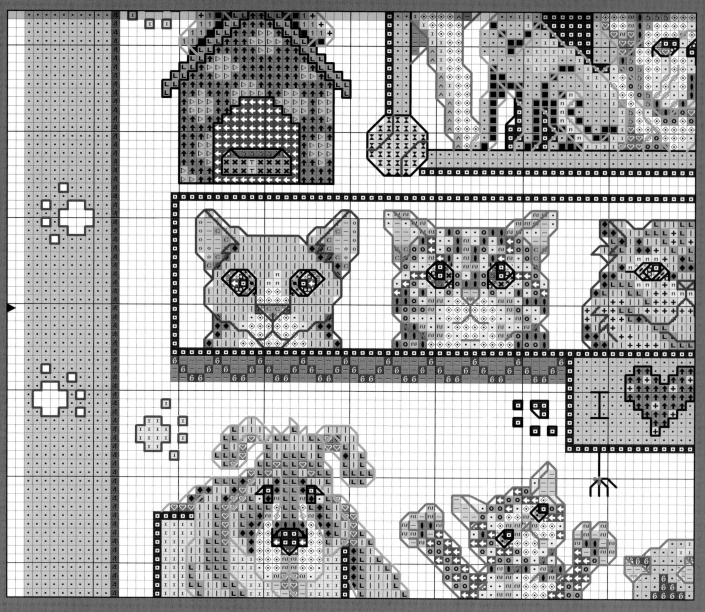

All Creatures Great and Small

DMC	X	1/4	BS	FK		DMC	X	1/4	BS	FK
1	◈	◈				472	H			
166	Z					726	X	X		
310	▣	▣	╱	•		738	•	•		
318	o	o				739	I	I		
350	↑	↑				742	▱	▱		
352	▷					746	n	n		
402	a					762	•	•		
413	←	←	╱			825	◪	◪	╱	
414	◖	◖				827	T	T		
415	∾	∾				898	6	6	╱	
435	■	■								

Grayed stitches indicate last row from previous section of design.

All Creatures Great and Small

DMC	X	1/4	BS	FK
899	C	C		
906	−	−		
907	◣	◢		
921	◆			
922	L	L		
975	4	4	✎	
977	1	1		
3716	−	−		
3778	5	5		
3779	o	o		

DMC	X	1/4	BS	FK
3825	I	I		
3826	▪	▪		
3830	♡	♡		
3844	3	3		
3846	✖	×		
3855	+			
3858	◤	◤		
3862	▶			
3863	−	−		
3864	∧	∧		

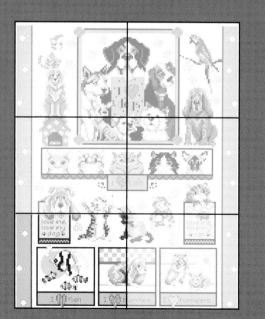

All Creatures Great and Small

DMC	X	1/4	BS	FK
1	◈	◈		
166	Z			
310	▣	▣	╱	●
318	◉	◉		
350	▲	▲		
352	▷			
402	α			
413	◀	◀	╱	
414	◖	◖		
415	∿	∿		
435	■	■		

DMC	X	1/4	BS	FK
472	H			
726	✕	✕		
738	▪	▪		
739	I	I		
742	╱	╱		
746	n	n		
762	▪	▪		
825	◪	◪	╱	
827	T	T		
898	6	6	╱	

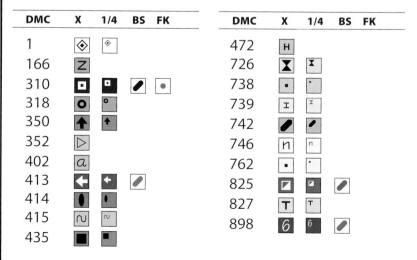

Grayed stitches indicate last row from previous section of design.

love me, love my cat

unnies   I ❤ hamsters

All Creatures Great and Small

DMC	X	1/4	BS	FK
899	C	C		
906	–	–		
907	◣	◣		
921	◆			
922	L	L		
975	4	4		⬭
977	1	1		
3716	–	–		
3778	5	5		
3779	o	o		

DMC	X	1/4	BS	FK
3825	I	I		
3826	▪	▪		
3830	♡	♡		
3844	3	3		
3846	✖	×		
3855	✚			
3858	◢	◢		
3862	▶			
3863	–	–		
3864	∧	^		

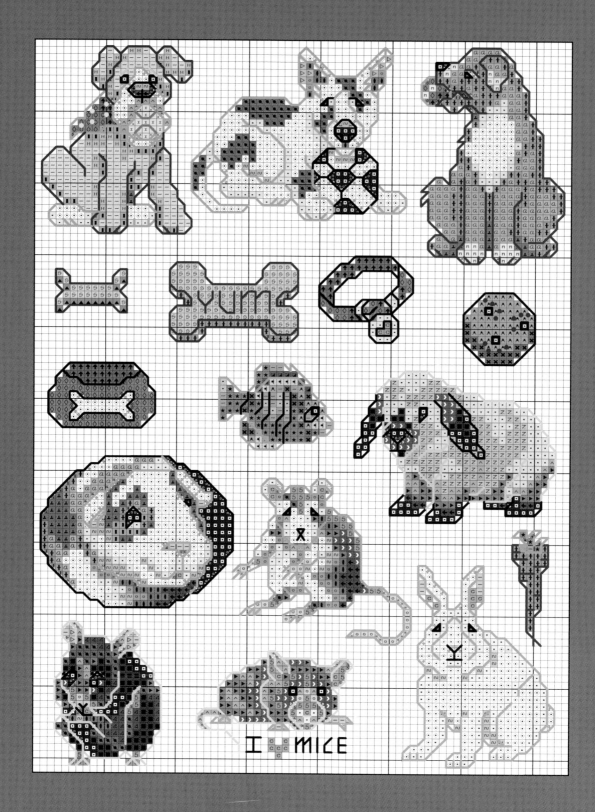

I ♥ MICE

All Creatures Great and Small
Alternate Designs

DMC	X	1/4	BS	FK	DMC	X	1/4	BS	FK	DMC	X	1/4	BS	FK	DMC	X	1/4
1	◈	◈	╱	•	472	•				906	★	★			3827	H	
304	⬆	⬆			726	I	I			907	—	—			3830	◣	◣
310	▣	▣	╱	•	738	Z				922	✚	✚			3844	✖	✖
318	○	○			739	•	•			975	4	4	╱		3846	▲	▲
350	◇	◇			746	n	n			977	▮	▮			3855	—	—
352	▷	▷			762	•	•			3716	—	—			3856	6	6
402	a	a			825	◢				3776	▲	▲			3858	❯	❯
413	◀	◀	╱		827	◀	◀			3778	5	5			3863	▶	▶
414	⬮	⬮			898	■	■	╱		3779	○	○			3864	∧	∧
415	∿	∿			899	C	C			3826	⬛	⬛	╱				

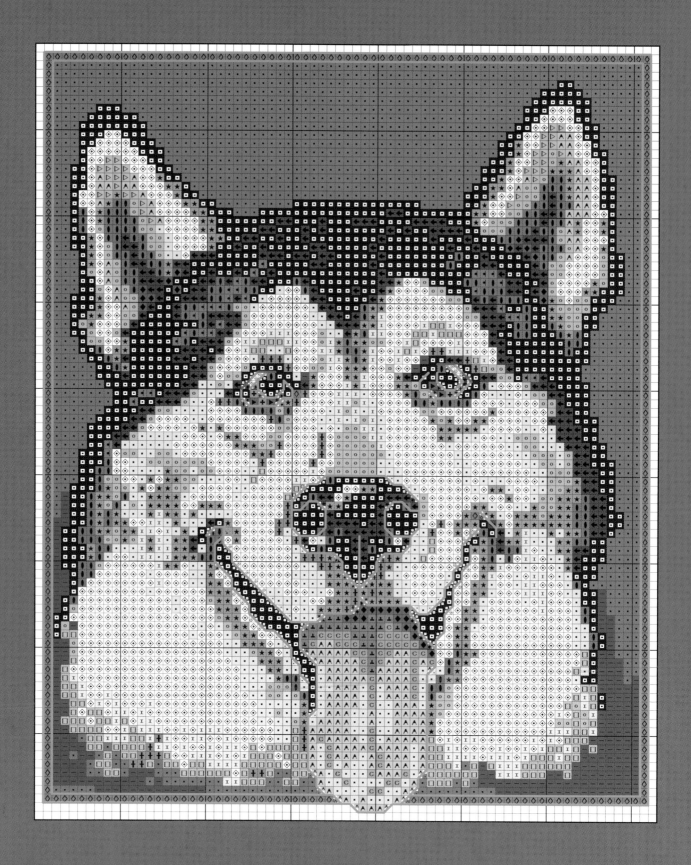

All Creatures Great and Small
Alternate Designs

DMC	X	1/4	BS		DMC	X	1/4		DMC	X	1/4		DMC	X	1/4		DMC	X	1/4
1	◈	◈	▱		414	◗	◗		792	▬			975	◤			3827	H	
310	▣	▣	▱		415	○			799	✛	✛		975	◣			3830	▶	▶
318	★	★			434	♥	♥		898	■	■		3325	▢	▢		3838	▪	▪
333	⬆	⬆			435	L	L		899	C			3350	◆	◆		3856	△	△
350	◇	◇			436	n	n		921	▮			3716	▲	^		3858	▶	▶
352	▷				562	▪			922	✚	✚		3731	⊥	⊥		3863	◀	◀
402	✖				762	▪	▫		951	I	I		3776	▲			3864	^	^
413	◀	◀	▱		775	I			963	▪	▫		3778	5	5				

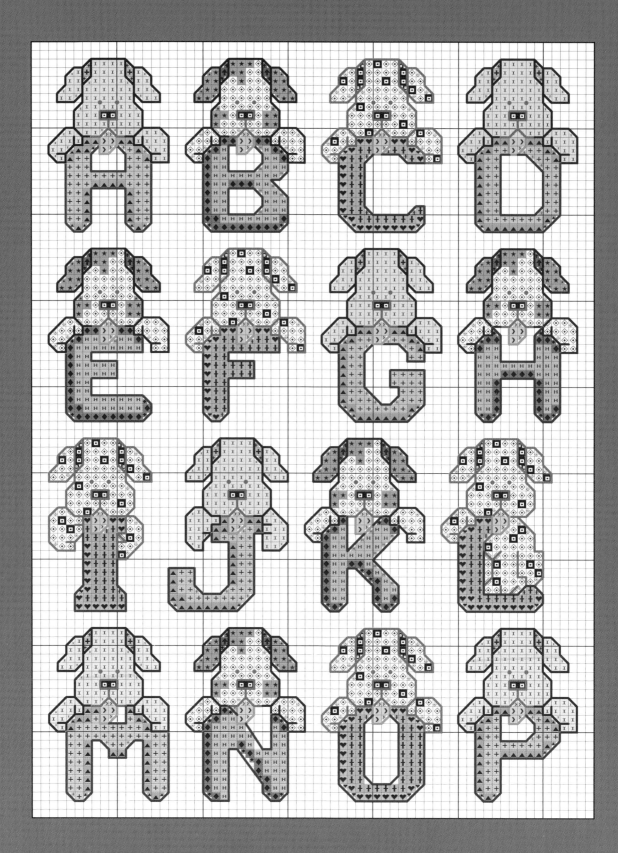

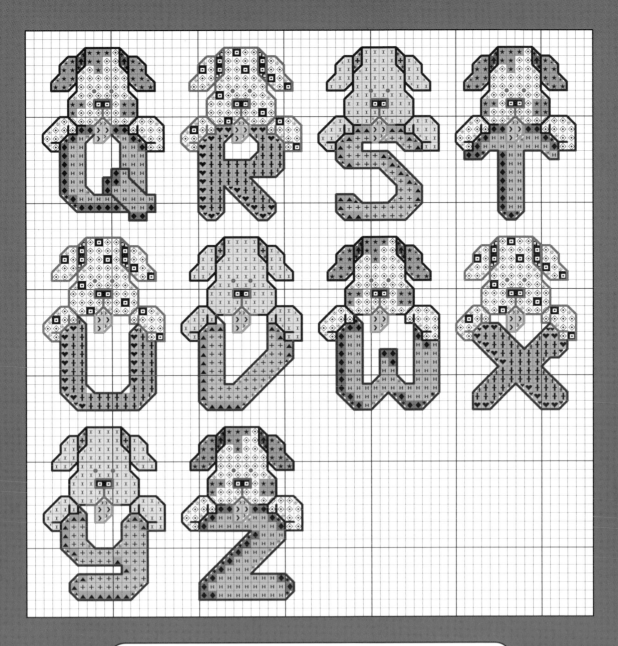

All Creatures Great and Small
Alternate Designs

DMC	X	1/4	BS	FK	DMC	X	1/4	BS	FK
1	◈	◈			504	H	H		
301	▲	▲			602			⁄	
310	▣	▣	⁄	•	776	❭	❭		
317			⁄		800	✚	✚		
433			⁄		809	▲	▲		
436	★	★			951	I	I		
437	✚	✚			3609	❤	❤		
502	◆	◆			3727	✚	✚		

HOME
FOR THE HOLIDAYS

Home for the Holidays

Size: 149w x 191h
Fabric: 14 ct. Charles Craft, Beige

DMC	X	BS	FK	DMC	X	BS	FK
1	◇	╱		436	2		
221	♡			501	◩		
341	4			502	◇		
347	◣	⬭		503	H		
351	n			535	✗		
352	◣			646	�há		
434	⚓	⬭		647	5		
435	╱			648	⌘		

Grayed stitches indicate last row from previous section of design.

Home for the Holidays

DMC	X	BS	FK	DMC	X	BS	FK
744	—			3345	◣	◢	
758	▷			3346	◭		
798	◻	◢		3347	◿		
799	◿			3348	C		
801	∧		•	3371	+	◢	•
945	○			3747	T		
3064	▣			3766	◺		
3072	✓			3854	★		

Home for the Holidays

DMC	X	BS	FK	DMC	X	BS	FK
1	◇	▱		436	2		
221	♡			501	◪		
341	4			502	◇		
347	◪	▱		503	H		
351	n			535	◪		
352	◣			646	◣		
434	⚓	▱		647	5		
435	⁄			648	⌘		

Personalization Line

Grayed stitches indicate last row from previous section of design.

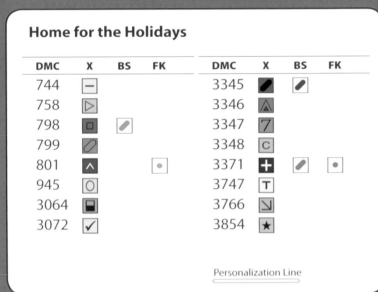

Home for the Holidays

DMC	X	BS	FK		DMC	X	BS	FK
744	—				3345			
758					3346			
798					3347			
799					3348			
801			•		3371	+		•
945					3747			
3064					3766			
3072					3854	★		

Personalization Line

Home for the Holidays

DMC	X	BS	FK	DMC	X	BS	FK
1	◈	◨		436	2		
221	♡			501	◪		
341	4			502	◇		
347	◥	◓		503	H		
351	n			535	⬙		
352	◥			646	◥		
434	⚓	◗		647	5		
435	◢			648	⌘		

ER AND THROUGH
UODDS TO
ER'S HOUSE WE GO

Home for the Holidays

DMC	X	BS	FK		DMC	X	BS	FK
744	—				3345	◣	◢	
758	▷				3346	◬		
798	◙	◢			3347	◸		
799	◿				3348	C		
801	⌃		•		3371	✚	◢	•
945	○				3747	T		
3064	▣				3766	↘		
3072	✓				3854	★		

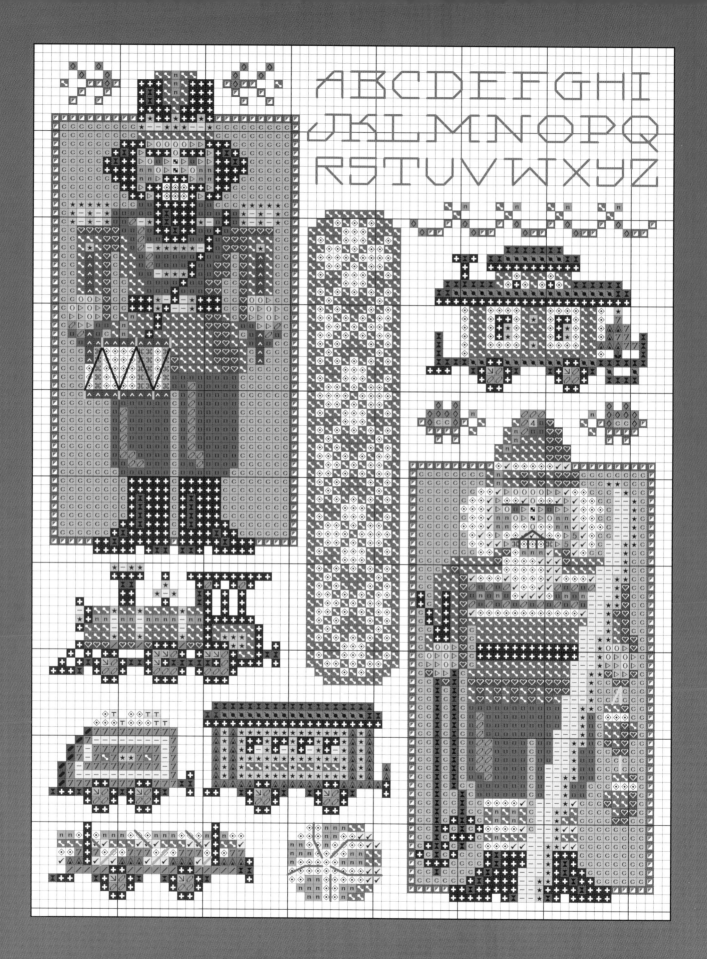

Home for the Holidays
Alternate Designs

DMC	X	BS	FK	STR	DMC	X	BS	FK	STR	DMC	X	BS	FK	STR
1	◈				535	▨	✎ *			3072	✓			
221	♥			✎ *	646	◣				3345	◪			
341	4				647	5				3346	◮	✎ *		
347	◣	✎ *			648	⌘				3347	7			
351	n				744	—				3348	C			
352	◣		•		758	▷				3371	+	✎ *	•	
434	⬇				798	▢		✎ *		3747	T			
435	/				799	/				3766	↘			
501	◪				801	∧				3854	★			✎ *
502	◇				945	○								
503	H				951	◪								

*2-ply

109

Home for the Holidays
Alternate Designs

DMC	X	BS	FK
1	◈		
221	♥		
341	4		
347	◣		•
351	n		
352	◣		
434	⚓	◪ *	•
435	◿		

DMC	X	BS	FK
436	2		
501	◪		
502	◇		
503	H		
535	✖		
646	◣		
647	5		
648	⌘		

DMC	X	BS	FK
744	—		
758	▷		
798	□		
799	◿		
801	⋀		
945	○		
3072	✓		
3345	◪		

DMC	X	BS	FK
3346	▲		
3347	7		
3348	C		
3371	✚	◪ *	•
3854	★		

*2-ply

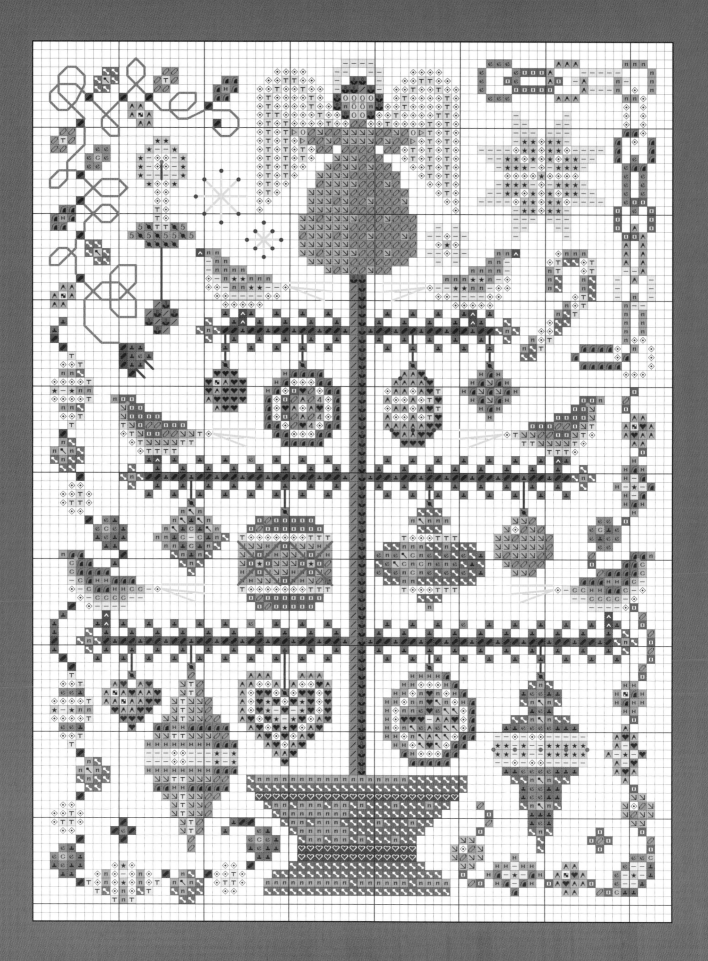

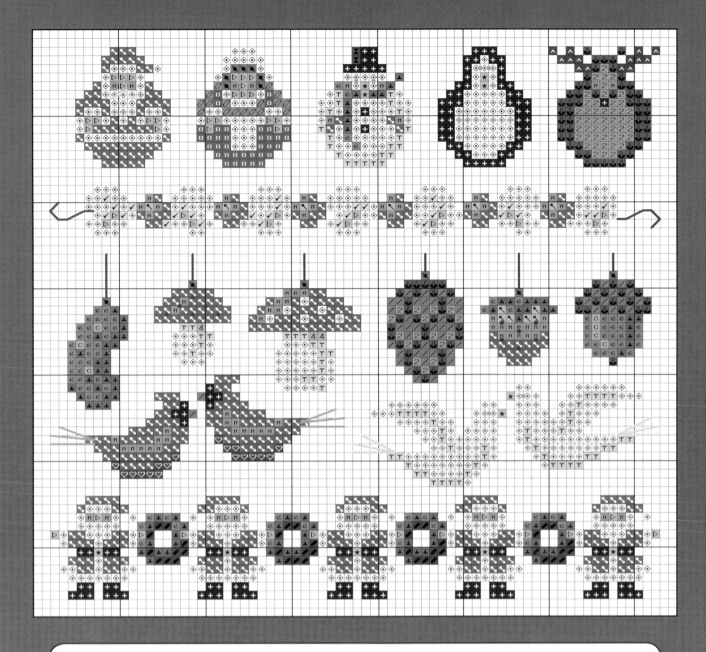

Home for the Holidays
Alternate Designs

DMC	X	BS	FK	STR	DMC	X	BS	FK	STR	DMC	X	BS	FK	STR
1	◇		• *	⟋ *	535	⊠	⟋ *			951	◪			
208	◪				602	♥				987	⊥		• #	
209	H				603	⋀				988	e			
221	♥				646	◣				3072	✓			
341	4				647	5				3345	◢	⟋ *		
347	◥			⟋ *	744	—			⟋ *	3348	C			
351	n		•		758	▷				3371	+		• #	
352	◣				798	▫				3747	T			
434	⚓				799	⟋				3766	↘			
435	⟋				801	⋀				3854	★			
436	2				945	⊙								

*2-ply
3-Ply

ALPHABET
GARDEN

Alphabet Garden

Size: 141w x 191h

Fabric: 14 ct. Charles Craft, White

DMC	X	BS	FK	DMC	X	BS	FK
1	◈			772	△		
153	4			839	▣	▱	•
209	◣			839		▱*	
471	◉			910	★		
472	7			912	m		
518	▲			954	C		
519	•			3078	□		
553	✖			3326	ⲓ		

*2-ply

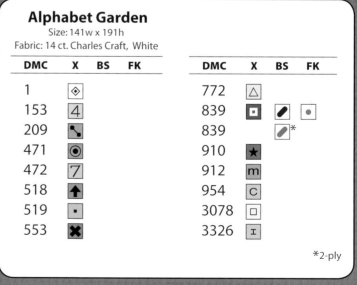

Grayed stitches indicate last row from previous section of design.

Alphabet Garden

DMC	X	BS	FK		DMC	X	BS	FK
3346	◆				3855	a		
3607	♥	✎			3862	✎		
3761	❯				3863	⋈		
3806	n				3864	T		
3853	✕							
3854	⊥							

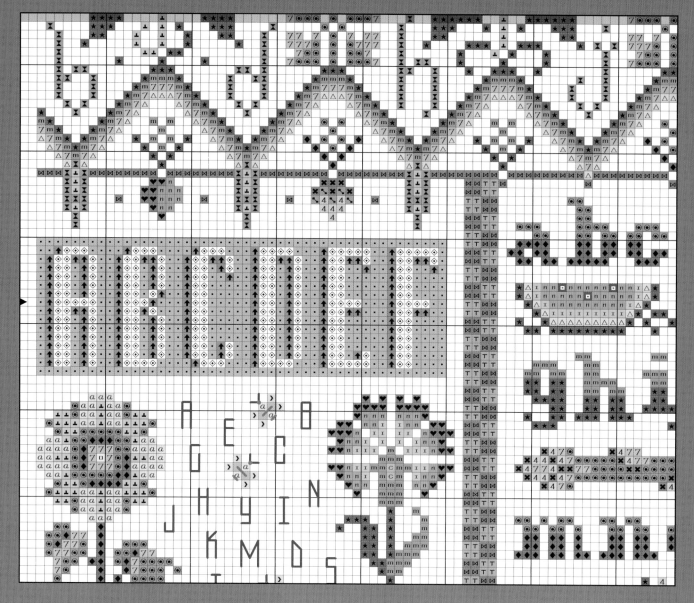

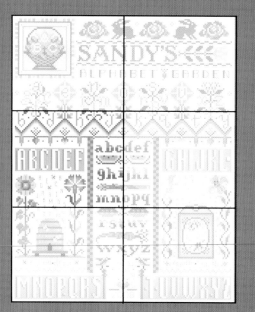

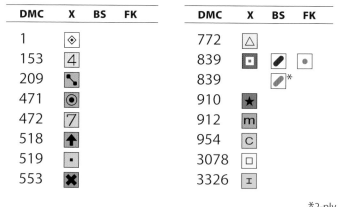

Alphabet Garden

DMC	X	BS	FK	DMC	X	BS	FK
1	◈			772	△		
153	4			839	▣	✎	•
209	◣			839		✎ *	
471	◉			910	★		
472	7			912	m		
518	⬆			954	C		
519	•			3078	□		
553	✖			3326	ɪ		

*2-ply

Grayed stitches indicate last row from previous section of design.

Alphabet Garden

DMC	X	BS	FK
3346	◆		
3607	♥	✎	
3761	❭		
3806	n		
3853	✕		
3854	⊥		

DMC	X	BS	FK
3855	a		
3862	✐		
3863	⋈		
3864	T		

Bottom Left

ALPHA·BEES

Alphabet Garden

DMC	X	BS	FK		DMC	X	BS	FK
1	◈				772	△		
153	4				839	▣	◗	•
209	◣				839		◗*	
471	⊙				910	★		
472	7				912	m		
518	↑				954	C		
519	·				3078	□		
553	✖				3326	ɪ		

*2-ply

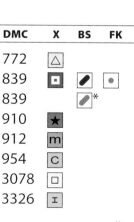

Grayed stitches indicate last row from previous section of design.

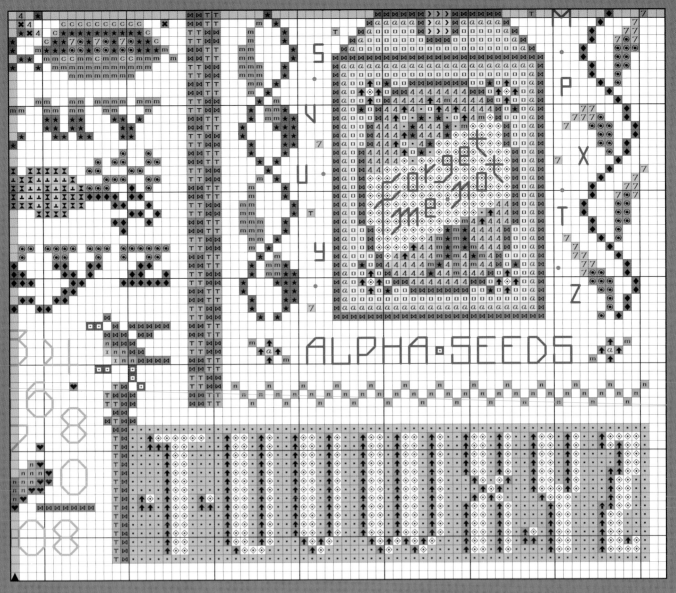

Alphabet Garden

DMC	X	BS	FK		DMC	X	BS	FK
3346	◆				3855	a		
3607	♥	✎			3862	◣		
3761	❯				3863	⋈		
3806	n				3864	T		
3853	✗							
3854	⊥							

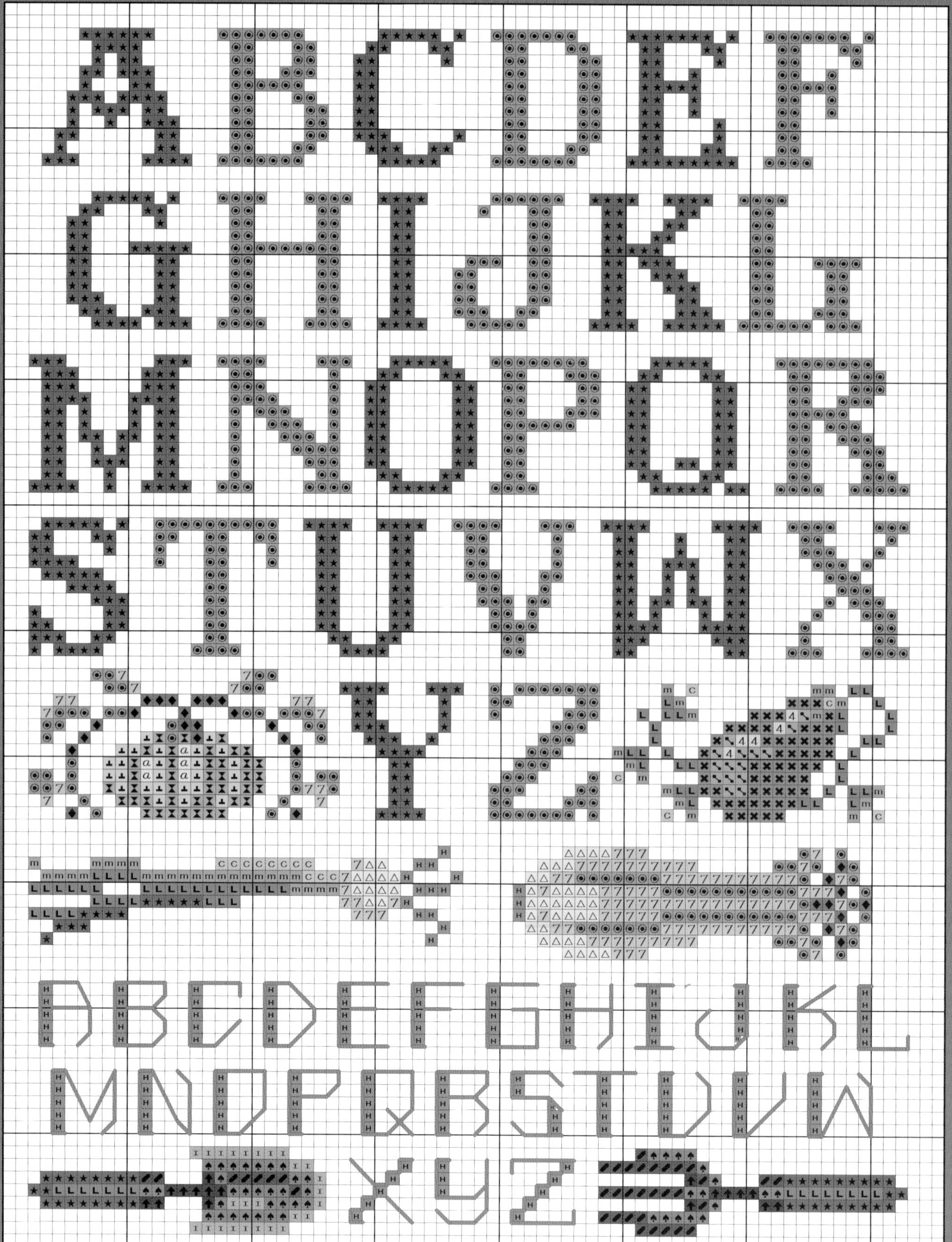

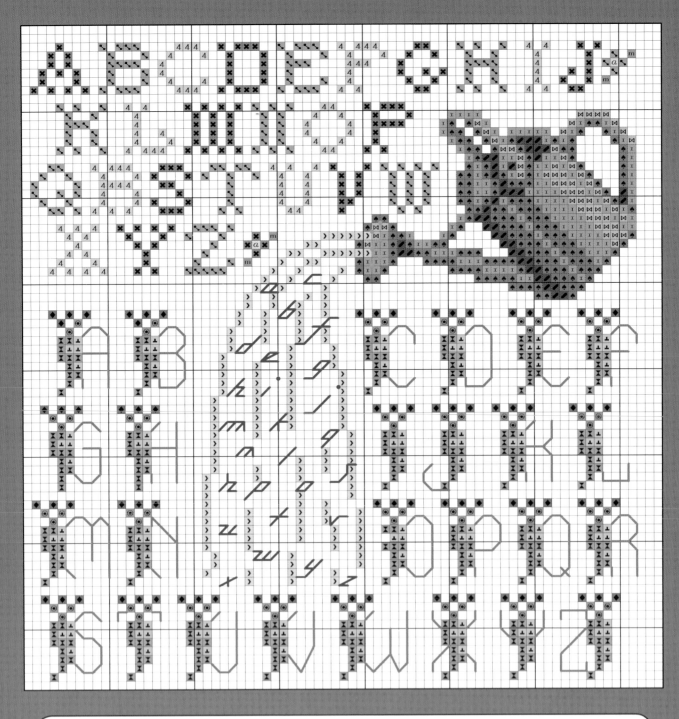

Alphabet Garden

Alternate Designs

DMC	X	1/4	BS	FK
153	4			
209	◥			
318	I			
413	◣			●
414	♠			
415	⋈			

DMC	X	1/4	BS	FK
471	⊙			
472	7			
553	✖			
772	△			
838	⬆		◢	●
839			◢*	
910	★			
911	L			

DMC	X	1/4	BS	FK
912	m			
954	c			
3346	◆			
3761	❭			
3853	✗			
3854	⊥			
3855	a			
3863	H	H		

*2-ply

ANCHOR CONVERSION CHART

DMC	ANCHOR	DMC	ANCHOR	DMC	ANCHOR	DMC	ANCHOR	DMC	ANCHOR
B5200	1	367	216	550	101	718	88	799	145
White	2	368	214	552	99	720	325	800	144
Ecru	387	369	1043	553	98	721	324	801	359
208	110	370	888	554	95	722	323	806	169
209	109	371	887	561	212	725	305	807	168
210	108	372	887	562	210	726	295	809	130
211	342	400	351	563	208	727	293	813	161
221	897	402	1047	564	206	729	890	814	45
223	895	407	914	580	924	730	845	815	44
224	893	413	236	581	281	731	281	816	43
225	1026	414	235	597	1064	732	281	817	13
300	352	415	398	598	1062	733	280	818	23
301	1049	420	374	600	59	734	279	819	271
304	19	422	372	601	63	738	361	820	134
307	289	433	358	602	57	739	366	822	390
309	42	434	310	603	62	740	316	823	152
310	403	435	365	604	55	741	304	824	164
311	148	436	363	605	1094	742	303	825	162
312	979	437	362	606	334	743	302	826	161
315	1019	444	291	608	330	744	301	827	160
316	1017	445	288	610	889	745	300	828	9159
317	400	451	233	611	898	746	275	829	906
318	235	452	232	612	832	747	158	830	277
319	1044	453	231	613	831	754	1012	831	277
320	215	469	267	632	936	758	9575	832	907
321	47	470	266	640	393	760	1022	833	874
322	978	471	265	642	392	761	1021	834	874
326	59	472	253	644	391	762	234	838	1088
327	101	498	1005	645	273	772	259	839	1086
333	119	500	683	646	8581	775	128	840	1084
334	977	501	878	647	1040	776	24	841	1082
335	40	502	877	648	900	778	968	842	1080
336	150	503	876	666	46	780	309	844	1041
340	118	504	206	676	891	781	308	869	375
341	117	517	162	677	361	782	308	890	218
347	1025	518	1039	680	901	783	307	891	35
349	13	519	1038	699	923	791	178	892	33
350	11	520	862	700	228	792	941	893	27
351	10	522	860	701	227	793	176	894	26
352	9	523	859	702	226	794	175	895	1044
353	8	524	858	703	238	796	133	898	380
355	1014	535	401	704	256	797	132	899	38
356	1013	543	933	712	926	798	146	900	333

DMC	ANCHOR	DMC	ANCHOR	DMC	ANCHOR	DMC	ANCHOR	DMC	ANCHOR
902	897	961	76	3326	36	3761	928	3827	311
904	258	962	75	3328	1024	3765	170	3828	373
905	257	963	23	3340	329	3766	167	3829	901
906	256	964	185	3341	328	3768	779	3830	5975
907	255	966	240	3345	268	3770	1009	Variegated Colors	
909	923	970	925	3346	267	3772	1007	48	1207
910	230	971	316	3347	266	3773	1008	51	1220
911	205	972	298	3348	264	3774	778	52	1209
912	209	973	290	3350	77	3776	1048	53	——
913	204	975	357	3354	74	3777	1015	57	1203
915	1029	976	1001	3362	263	3778	1013	61	1218
917	89	977	1002	3363	262	3779	868	62	1201
918	341	986	246	3364	261	3781	1050	67	1212
919	340	987	244	3371	382	3782	388	69	1218
920	1004	988	243	3607	87	3787	904	75	1206
921	1003	989	242	3608	86	3790	904	90	1217
922	1003	991	1076	3609	85	3799	236	91	1211
924	851	992	1072	3685	1028	3801	1098	92	1215
926	850	993	1070	3687	68	3802	1019	93	1210
927	849	995	410	3688	75	3803	69	94	1216
928	274	996	433	3689	49	3804	63	95	1209
930	1035	3011	856	3705	35	3805	62	99	1204
931	1034	3012	855	3706	33	3806	62	101	1213
932	1033	3013	853	3708	31	3807	122	102	1209
934	862	3021	905	3712	1023	3808	1068	103	1210
935	861	3022	8581	3713	1020	3809	1066	104	1217
936	846	3023	899	3716	25	3810	1066	105	1218
937	268	3024	388	3721	896	3811	1060	106	1203
938	381	3031	905	3722	1027	3812	188	107	1203
939	152	3032	898	3726	1018	3813	875	108	1220
943	189	3033	387	3727	1016	3814	1074	111	1218
945	881	3041	871	3731	76	3815	877	112	1201
946	332	3042	870	3733	75	3816	876	113	1210
947	330	3045	888	3740	872	3817	875	114	1213
948	1011	3046	887	3743	869	3818	923	115	1206
950	4146	3047	852	3746	1030	3819	278	121	1210
951	1010	3051	845	3747	120	3820	306	122	1215
954	203	3052	844	3750	1036	3821	305	123	——
955	203	3053	843	3752	1032	3822	295	124	1210
956	40	3064	883	3753	1031	3823	386	125	1213
957	50	3072	397	3755	140	3824	8	126	1209
958	187	3078	292	3756	1037	3825	323		
959	186	3325	129	3760	162	3826	1049		

ABOUT THE AUTHOR

IN HER 34 YEARS OF EXPERIENCE in the needlework field—12 as a design director and 22 as the head of her own business—Donna Kooler has nurtured the talents of many gifted individuals. She is the president of Kooler Design Studio, Inc., located in Pleasant Hill, California, and above all else, her job is to inspire her staff to "produce the highest quality designs available in the marketplace and to exceed their customers' expectations."

Under Donna's direction, Kooler Design Studio produces needlework, craft, knitting, crochet, quilting, and painting kits, leaflets, and hardcover books. The studio and its designers have won numerous awards, including the Outstanding Award of Excellence from P.J.S. Publishing, the Golden Needle Award, and numerous Charted Designer of America Awards.

At the core of Kooler Design Studio, Inc., is a talented staff of designers: Linda Gillum, Nancy Rossi, Sandy Orton, and Barbara Baatz Hillman. Linda Gillum is co-founder and executive vice president of Kooler Design Studio. She's an award-winning designer and a fine artist—her talent is expressed in all design disciplines. Sandy Orton, designer and expert on adapting old artwork into needlework, is adept in the use of specialty stitches and creates historically correct samplers as well as wonderful Victorian stitchery pieces.

Even after three decades, every day is still an adventure for Donna, and Kooler Design Studio now includes a second generation of creative Koolers: Donna and her daughter Basha are now working side by side. Can life be any sweeter?

ACKNOWLEDGMENTS

AS EACH BOOK is about to be handed over to the publisher, I look back at the process, and I'm amazed at how much effort and talent, by so many, goes into each project.

First and foremost, I wish to thank Linda Gillum, Sandy Orton, and Barbara Baatz Hillman for their extraordinary artistic talent and beautiful designs. I am grateful for their dedication to making Kooler Design Studio an outstanding design team.

My thanks to the whole Kooler Design Studio staff who charted, stitched, proofed, proofed, and re-proofed this book, as well as the support we have received from the people at Lark Books. When creative people choose to work together, they can do awesome things.

METRIC CONVERSION CHART

INCHES	MILLIMETERS(mm)/ CENTIMETERS(cm)	INCHES	MILLIMETERS(mm)/ CENTIMETERS(cm)
1/8	3 mm	15	38.1 cm
3/16	5 mm	15½	39.4 cm
1/4	6 mm	16	40.6 cm
5/16	8 mm	16½	41.9 cm
7/8	9.5 mm	17	43.2 cm
7/16	1.1 cm	17½	44.5 cm
1/2	1.3 cm	18	45.7 cm
9/16	1.4 cm	18½	47 cm
5/8	1.6 cm	19	48.3 cm
11/16	1.7 cm	19½	49.5 cm
3/4	1.9 cm	20	50.8 cm
13/16	2.1 cm	20½	52 cm
7/8	2.2 cm	21	53.3 cm
15/16	2.4 cm	21½	54.6 cm
1	2.5 cm	22	55 cm
1½	3.8 cm	22½	57.2 cm
2	5 cm	23	58.4 cm
2½	6.4 cm	23½	59.7 cm
3	7.6 cm	24	61 cm
3½	8.9 cm	24½	62.2 cm
4	10.2 cm	25	63.5 cm
4½	11.4 cm	25½	64.8 cm
5	12.7 cm	26	66 cm
5½	14 cm	26½	67.3 cm
6	15.2 cm	27	68.6 cm
6½	16.5 cm	27½	69.9 cm
7	17.8 cm	28	71.1 cm
7½	19 cm	28½	72.4 cm
8	20.3 cm	29	73.7 cm
8½	21.6 cm	29½	74.9 cm
9	22.9 cm	30	76.2 cm
9½	24.1 cm	30½	77.5 cm
10	25.4 cm	31	78.7 cm
10½	26.7 cm	31½	80 cm
11	27.9 cm	32	81.3 cm
11½	29.2 cm	32½	82.6 cm
12	30.5 cm	33	83.8 cm
12½	31.8 cm	33½	85 cm
13	33 cm	34	86.4 cm
13½	34.3 cm	34½	87.6 cm
14	35.6 cm	35	88.9 cm
14½	36.8 cm	35½	90.2 cm
		36	91.4 cm

INDEX

Conversion chart
    Anchor, 124
    Metric, 127
Design
    Centering, 8
    Finished size, 8
    Linda Gillum, 36, 50, 62, 86
    Sandy Orton, 22, 76, 100
Fabric
    Cleaning, 8
    Preparing, 8
Floss
    Carrying, 8
    Securing, 8
Needles, 8
Stitches
    Backstitch, 9
    Colonial knot, 9
    Cross stitch, 9
    Fractional cross, 9
    French knot, 9
    Half cross, 9
    Straight, 9